Warriors M

Poems and Songs of the Warrior

By Steve Rowe

Published By Shi Kon

www.shikon.com

Copyright © 2015 by Steve Rowe

ISBN 978-1-326-36042-9

Cover photo by Michael Townsend of Loki photography

Table of Contents

Introduction

I've tried to produce this book in the simplest way possible to get to as many students, friends and social media followers as I can.

Thick technical books don't get read, simple poetry and prose does. I'm not aiming for the head but for the heart. I meditated for 52 days and wrote one poem during each meditation, these came straight from my heart and are written directly how I talk to myself. Anyone that knows me or is following me on social media will have watched me doing this and many have asked for them to be recorded in print so that they can keep and refer to them.

If you want to understand the Shi Kon training system, reading this book and meditating on the contents is the best way to do it. We practice a martial art and the 'art' means that it cannot be appreciated just in words and logic. Poetry is also an art and can bypass linear thinking to bring a 'glimpse' of what cannot usually be described in words.

I have not put them in a specific order on purpose. I would like you to read them randomly and then meditate on the contents, re-read the poem during the day and allow the ideas to 'hang' in your mind. Enlightenment as to the meaning will come as the ideas percolate in your subconscious.

Our training system is the search for wisdom. We want to live our life from the inside out instead of being manipulated from the outside in. To do this we must meditate, consider and challenge everything we encounter each day so that all ideas and principles are the ones that we have decided after careful consideration.

I hope that these ideas will trigger yours, that they will help you change your life in a positive way. The true way of the warrior.

A Black Belt

This is the most talked about subject in the martial arts,
Mention 'black belt' on social media and there is a tirade,
Everyone wants to have his or her say,
And tell how hard it was to get their grade.

I used to think everyone could be a black belt.
The 'way' was simple,
All they had to do was train every day for 3 – 5 yrs,
Attend 2 or 3 lessons a week,
Pay attention to instruction,
And they would make the grade.

Over the years I realised that was not true.
Many won't make it as long as they have a hole in their backside.
Some are just scared of the responsibility of being good,
Some are scared of their spouses and family,
Who don't want a stronger version of them.

Some are just so weak willed they don't have it in them.
Most people blame the Instructor,
Or family or work commitments,
Or their relationship with other students,
Or that 'the boss' (their spouse) won't let them.

Or nagging injury or illness,

Not realising that overcoming these problems is what makes a black belt.

Some give up when they get the grade.

Not realising that is also a test.

Black belt means beginner,

It only means that you've found the ladder to climb.

'Snatching defeat from the jaws of victory' describes them well.

A black belt is an investment in a person.

It is only a belt and a piece of paper

Wearing it is another thing.

Many martial artists don't realise they failed at that point.

Taking responsibility for themselves,

Their own training,

Their own standards,

Their own progress,

Never blaming others for a setback,

Being strong enough to help others,

THAT's a black belt.

Losing The Way

What does 'culture' do?
A baby sits and stands true,
They walk from the middle,
The world plays with them;
They are not separate from all around,
They smile easily,
Until they learn their name.

Others tell them who they are,
What they are like,
What they should be like;
School indoctrinates them as political slaves,
Who they really are starts to fade,
As a false identity is assumed.

Who are you? I am my name,
My job is, my car is, and my hobbies are,
I am confused.

Why can't these people tell what their body is doing?
Why can't they have pure intention?
Why are they so emotionally troubled?
Why can't they 'just do' Kung Fu?
They had it as a baby,
And then they lost the 'Way'...

Internal Or External

Internal and external has many translations in the Martial Arts,

You cannot be one or the other,

Because we all have an inside and an outside,

If you are more one than the other, you are unbalanced.

If you're taught externally,

Your instructor will correct you by how you look on the outside:

If you're taught internally,

Your instructor will correct you by how you feel inside.

Ideally, you need both.

If you train externally,

You will utilise the power of emotion,

If you train internally,

Your mind will be calm and focused.

If you train externally,

You will use the outer muscles in small combinations,

If you train internally,

You will use the deep muscles and spine,

All connected and moving in harmony.

The deep muscles and spine hold emotion.

They also support the internal organs.

Softening and correcting them,

Will increase health and vitality.

Many martial arts go from more external to internal.

Some from more internal to external.

It's always good to train both in balance.

Because you can't have just an inside or outside.

When you move one you always move the other.

Before Everything

Step into the 'psychic elevator'.
Some go up, I go down.
Dropping like a stone.
Down, down I go.

Past structured thoughts and words;
Way past feelings and emotions;
Beyond 'self'.
I'm into my DNA

Down through the generations;
Prehistoric man,
Mammals, back into the sea;
Single cell, before the primordial soup.

The planets gather and roll back,
The Universe implodes;
What is there?
Nothing - no thing.

So I sit in no thingness,
What we and all matter were before;
Joined with everything in no thingness;
In beforeness, healing, nourishing;
Feeling the energy build up in purity...

Before the universe farted.

The Training Bank

Be a saver not a spender.

Every training session good or bad,

Is a penny in the Training Bank.

Day after day,

Weeks after week,

Year after year,

The pennies accumulate;

Until you have great martial arts wealth.

Every seminar, course and lesson adds to the value.

Every note you take,

Every time you pay attention,

Everything you contribute to your teacher and classmates,

A penny drops in.

Every meditation,

Every time you stand straight,

Every time you breathe deep,

Every time you focus your mind,

Another penny drops in.

Bit by bit your power comes from within,

And you're not so influenced by what's without;

Eventually your martial wealth is yours to own.

The mortgage is paid.

A Door Inside

There is a door inside, in the deepest part of your heart.
When you exit this world, it closes behind you.
But it's a door that can be used for refuge at anytime.

Beyond it is a place of healing.
Nourishment for the soul,
A place where wisdom resides,
A land of language without words.

How do we find this door?
There is only one way,
Complete and utter stillness,
Death within life.

Thinking without words.
When you are still and there is no words,
Then the door will be felt.

Once inside, you can heal,
Understand what you were and will be,
The door remains open,
Always there for you to find.

Until the last time.

When the last breath is exhaled,

When the last thought passes
And the door closes on this body forever.

Zombie Or Alive?

It was a slow death....
That's impossible.
One second you're alive, the next you're dead.
Alive/dead; it's as simple as that.
You might be ill or in pain for a while;
But death is instantaneous.

Awake, asleep, you don't notice.
You only know you fell asleep when you awake.
As the anaesthetist puts the canula in your arm,
"Goodnight" and you're gone,
You only know you were gone when you're in recovery.

So dying is not a problem, one second you're alive and next you're not.
In meditation or everyday life you are aware and focused,
And then the mind has wandered.
You had a 'mini death';
Some people are never aware and focused;
They are zombies.

The better you meditate,
The more mindful you become,
The more you are alive.
Aware and focused or zombie?
Your choice.

It's A Kind of Magic

A Magi is a wise person,
Magic is knowing how something works.
Magic fools the ignorant,
Because it's 'special power' they don't understand,
But to the wise it's normal science.

Does this make magic less?
Should we not be in awe of the 'ordinary'?
Is not every day astounding?
The sun rising and setting,
The fact that we exist?
Earth, water, air and fire are all magical;
Every breath we take should inspire us with awe.

We know how it works,
We know the 'trick';
We become wise to what's happening;
But we should not become complacent.

Science should not make something less,
It should make it more.
When you break something down,
You can keep going infinitely.

When you build something up,
You can keep going infinitely.
Magical lore says 'as above, so below'.
It truly is awesome and a kind of magic.

Internal Or External

Internal and external has many translations in the Martial Arts,

You cannot be one or the other,

Because we all have an inside and an outside,

If you are more one than the other, you are unbalanced.

If you're taught externally,

Your instructor will correct you by how you look on the outside:

If you're taught internally,

Your instructor will correct you by how you feel inside.

Ideally, you need both.

If you train externally,

You will utilise the power of emotion,

If you train internally,

Your mind will be calm and focused.

If you train externally,

You will use the outer muscles in small combinations,

If you train internally,

You will use the deep muscles and spine,

All connected and moving in harmony.

The deep muscles and spine hold emotion.

They also support the internal organs.

Softening and correcting them,

Will increase health and vitality.

Many martial arts go from more external to internal.

Some from more internal to external.

It's always good to train both in balance.

Because you can't have just an inside or outside.

When you move one you always move the other.

Do The Dead Speak?

The dead are a part of us.

They live in our DNA.

The words they uttered are remembered,

They are written down,

Recorded and filmed.

DNA is changed by its environment.

Every action, thought and deed is recorded in it,

It's passed down through generations,

From the beginning of time.

We are a walking record of our forefathers,

And everything we have read, saw and heard in this life.

When we meditate, we gain mental clarity and sharpness,

What we need arises from this bank of information.

Innate wisdom resides in all of us,

If only we can still the mental clutter.

In stopping the influence from outside in,

And allowing the inside to come out,

Everything we need is there.

When we sit in stillness and ask 'is anybody there?'

An entire universe from the big bang onwards stirs,

We never were alone, we are emissaries of the dead.

The Stopped Breath...

Breathing crosses body barriers,
From sympathetic to parasympathetic,
We can control it with our mind,
When we don't, we breathe anyway.

It is a way to find zen,
A way to improve health,
A method to build power
And improve concentration.

Between breathing in and out,
And between out and in,
There is a magic Zen moment,
A moment in which we can access infinity.

We stop our breath to concentrate.
To draw a straight line freehand,
To listen intently,
Before we pee or poo,
And even before we vomit.
A moment of perfect Zen.

When we meditate, these are our magic moments.
Like the pauses between waves rolling in and out.
We learn to extend our Zen from these pauses.
And how to extend and deepen our breathing.

When in combat we can't match breath to technique.
So breathing has to be natural.
When we collide with the opponent,
Or when we need to focus,
We momentarily stop our breath.
For perfect concentrated Zen.

Stick A Needle In Your Eye

Stick a needle in your eye – that's suffering.

Unrequited love – that's suffering.

Watching loved one's in pain – that's suffering.

Poverty illness and hunger – that's suffering.

Growing old and ugly – that's suffering,

Not getting what you want – that's suffering.

Getting what you want, that's suffering…

Hang on – how can that be suffering?

Because the moment you get it, you try to keep it,

That new car as the mileage goes up isn't new anymore,

Every scratch, bit of dirt and use wears it away.

You don't have it – you suffer;

You have it – you suffer…

Whether you suffer or not depends on how you look at it,

It depends on your perspective.

If you are attracted to something – you suffer.

If you try to push it away – you suffer;

Attraction and aversion are the same,

Just two sides to the same coin.

How do you live and not suffer?

By changing your perspective.

Fully engage in life, but let it pass.

Nothing stays the same.

Life isn't fair.

Joy and pain only exist because of the other.

Each will pass in it's own time.

Live it, love it and let it go.

Give without the need to receive;

Always consider the needs of others,

And you will always be happy.

Heaven Or Hell
Is this heaven or hell?
Are the people around you stupid and ignorant?
Are they only out for themselves?
Are they all cheats and liars?
If so, you are in hell.

Are the people around you patient and tolerant?
Are they kind and supportive?
Do you all work as a team in a positive way?
Then you are in heaven.

Like attracts like.
Birds of a feather stick together.
You determine whether you are in heaven or hell.
It's your choice.

My Immortal Soul

Most of us are worried about what will happen to us when we die.
When all we have to do,
Is remember what we were before we were born.
What we are now, have always been,
And will always be.

Where is you immortal soul?
Why can't you feel it now?
Of course you can, it rests in your stillness.
Stand tall, breathe deep, focus your mind,
When the words stop and the body is still,
'You' cease to exist - and there it is.

It has no name, it pearmeates everything,
Everything within it rises and falls in time,
Hurt any part and you only hurt yourself,
Be kind to any part and you feel the reward.

This whole creation, this whole theatre,
Has but one purpose;
The reason you have 5 senses and a reflective conscious mind,
Is so that the universe, your immortal soul,
Can experience itself...

Inside Out

Are your techniques YouTube friendly?
Do they follow the 'fashion' of the day?
Do you 'train' or do you 'study?'
Do you pay lip service to meditation?
Or do you assiduously study it?

Are you the person that everyone thinks you are?
Are you your grade and qualifications?
Are you your career and car?
Are you how attractive you appear to others?
Are you the 'good guy' everyone says?

Are flattered by others?
Do you go with the 'zeitgeist' of opinion?
Do you work to 'fit in' and be popular?
Do you culture yourself to be accepted and praised?
Are you always looking for acceptance?
Then you have not followed the Warrior Way.

Or has your meditation and study made you a real person?
Do you work everything out for yourself?
Are your opinions properly considered and truly yours?
Do you understand the skills that really work?

Have you discarded the culture that others gave you?
And worked to find out who you really are?
Are you prepared to go against the grain?

To upset the 'popular' crowd?

To think and act from the inside out?

Have you become a true warrior of life?

And a "real' martial artist?

Blind Assumptions

Do you know what blind assumptions are?
They are the views and opinions that we grew up with,
They were always around us, our culture,
And we never knew they were there.

They came from our family,
They came from or friends,
They came from our schooling,
They came from our environment,
They were just always there.

We took them on board without knowing,
We naturally voice them as opinions,
We blindly accept them as a part of us,
Even though they never came from us.

They act as a barrier to the outside world,
We seek out like minded people,
People that 'are like us',
Even though they are not.

How do we find these assumptions?
Seek them out and change?
Firstly we have to go as deep as we can,
To discover who and what we really are.

Then we have to be mindful of everything we think and say,

To consider whether this is really our opinion,

To discover your blind assumptions can be a shock,

But from thereon you really can become yourself.

Blood On Wood

Thump, thump, thump...
He's out there again,
Hitting that bloody piece of wood in the garden,
One of those Kung Fu nutters.

Every bloody day it's the same,
Well I ain't gonna tell him,
He'll probably tie me up like a pretzel,
And post me back through our letterbox.

Thump, thump, thump,
Each time strike with seiken,
Shuto, tettsui and teisho,
Haito, koken and nukite.

Feet press directionally to the floor,
Spiraling through the legs,
Connecting through the core,
And powering out through the hands.

Thump, thump, thump,
The makiwara bends and is momentarily held,
The return force is repulsed,
Creating a 'double tap' of energy.

Thump thump thump,

Every day is a penny in the martial arts bank,

The blood on the wood is a reminder,

That everyone bleeds,

And all matter is impermanent.

Thump, thump, thump,

While life goes on we evolve,

Our resolve determination and courage,

Patience kindness and compassion,

Make us true martial art warriors…

One day there will be silence…

The makiwara will grow moss,

Nature will take it's course,

As all things pass…..

Bullying

Bullying is not always obvious,
Sometimes it's physical abuse,
Sometimes it's verbal and persuasive,
And sometimes it's on the screen you use.

The punching and kicking is obvious,
The name calling, taunting and rumour,
Destroying someone's reputation can be more hidden,
Done by nasty gossip and humour.

Recruiting others makes it seem legitimate,
Peer pressure makes it seem right,
When many agree to make one suffer,
Surely that makes it alright?

Bullies often have high social standing,
This empowers them with the crowd,
They are quick to be aggressive,
And the majority are scared to speak out.

The victim will be lonely and nervous,
And never seems to fit in,
The emotional damage is permanent,
And goes very deep within.

The bully will suffer the same,
But have learned to hide it well,
Be manipulative nasty and narcissistic,
And really as dark as hell.

To make sure we don't bully or assist,
We have to be emotionally secure,
Be ready to stand up for the bullied,
And not give in to our fear....

The Yin Factor

Men fight to protect their ego,
Women to protect their family,
Men beat their chests and shout,
Women prepare to be deadly.

Men move from the heart,
Women from the womb,
Men use their chest and shoulders,
Women their legs and middle.

Men use strength and power,
Women weapons and fluidity.
Men drink with their opponents after battle,
Women leave them dead.

Martial arts are more yin than yang,
They are quiet and deadly,
They use skill rather than force,
And are more defensive than offensive.

Martial arts rely on internal connection,
Their strength comes from the legs and core.
The quietness gives awareness and concentration,
And power from being sensitive and intense.

Do not mistake defensive for weak,
Power is in clarity and timing,
With no ego danger can be dealt with,
With deadly force if needed.

In martial arts training,
Men need to be more feminine,
Women more masculine,
But one doesn't need to become the other.

Martial Arts Are Defensive

'Budo' and 'Wu Shu' mean 'to stop the spear'.
In Iaido we have a reluctance to draw the sword.
'Satsu katsu' means 'life giving and life taking',
When forced to draw we kill.

'Karate Ni Sentenashi' means 'there is no first attack in karate'.
When forced to defend, we move decisively.
The Martial Arts are defensive,
But that does not make them weak.

Martial artists train every day,
Along with courage, resolve and determination,
We foster patience, kindness and compassion,
Martial arts training make us good people.

If the Martial Arts were aggressive,
That would make us weak, frightened people,
Like a snarling, scared dog sitting in the corner,
Having to intimidate every passer by.

Instead they make us emotionally intelligent,
Happy, relaxed and confident,
Able to foster good relationships,
And deal with situations where possible without violence.

If violence occurs we can deal with it decisively.

We do not fear the bully.

We are able to protect the weak,

As martial artists we are the 'Peacekeepers'.

Life's Not Fair…

Life's not fair,
It never was,
It's your life,
Deal with it.

God won't save you,
Neither will karma,
There is no lifeline,
You either swim or sink.

Life is a battle,
Your mind must be focused,
And always ready,
If it gets distracted,
You die.

When the warrior goes into battle,
If he thinks of home, he dies,
If he worries for the future, he dies,
He can only focus on the task in hand.

If he worries, he's killing himself.
If he's scared, he's killing himself.
If he blames others, he's killing himself.
Why would he do that?

The warrior deals with problems as they come along.

He maintains an unfettered mind.

That way he stands the best chance of survival.

If he fails, it's game over.

The Aliens have Landed!

The Aliens have landed!
The mysterious spaceship lands,
The leaders of humanity arrive to greet it,
At last, we get to know what's out there…

The crowds gather,
Everyone waits expectantly,
The doors 'woosh' open,
And perfectly circular beings roll out..

The Prime Minister steps forward and extends a hand,
The circle recoils, gathers itself and moves forwards;
"Sorry, your appearance is terrifying….
And I was taken aback."

"You have tentacles – and tentacles on tentacles,
Eyes that swivel and scary teeth when you smile.
You look shaven with ugly bits of hair in strange places and move strangely;
We evolved from something like you."

"But fear us not, we are here to help as an advanced species;
Our prime directive is not to interfere with the way you do things.
The way you treat each other and those beneath your evolved state,
Is the way that we will treat you."

Everyone seemed happy… they were here to help,

"The universe is a dangerous place and not everyone is friendly,

We will make sure you are protected as we have the means.

Those that may be dangerous, we will control."

"You kill each other without regard and anyone you see as a threat.

We will continue to do the same.

You breed, drug, confine and kill anything below your evolutionary state for food,

We will do the same… by the way we eat humans….."

"But fear not as we will treat you kindly.

You will be locked in a safe place,

Bred to be healthy and plump,

You will be killed humanely."

"You won't know what's happening because you're not as evolved as us,

Your species will survive because you're useful.

We will breed out any traits that don't fit in;

Just like you do to others now."

Gradually it dawned on the people watching,

That this was their new Government,

It would not be so different in the end even with the existing government,

Maybe they just wouldn't eat people….

Magpies and Monkeys

Ooohhh...... shiny object....
Damn.. I was supposed to be meditating,
Then I started thinking about that argument,
Then what I was having for dinner,
And then... oh well it doesn't matter.

How can I think of nothing?
Surely that's a thought in itself?
And if I don't know when my mind wanders,
How can I bring it back?

I feel like have a monkey on my back,
Always chattering in my ear,
Finding things for me to think about,
When I'm supposed to be concentrating on one thing.

Single whip again in Tai Chi, damn!
It occurs in the form so many times,
I stop and can't remember what technique comes next,
I was thinking about how to do it and not what's after.

There are so many interesting martial arts,
So many techniques to know,
So many ideas to know about,
What purpose can a 'still mind' have?

Don't think, feel, said Bruce Lee,
Do not think in words said Sifu,
Tai Chi is one thing, not many,
Wisdom lies in stillness.

A still body, a still mind,
Stillness in movement,
And movement in stillness.
Enter a small door, and penetrate deeply.

Keep it simple,
Be aware and focused,
Sensitive and intense,
Then the mind is sharp and guarded.

When you realise you're lost,
Dispassionately return,
Re-establish mindfulness,
And continue as if nothing happened.

Let the magpie go,
It was only your ego clinging on,
Cast off the monkey,
It was only misdirection.

They are illusion,
They crept in while mindfulness was absent,
They made your mind their home,
And now it's time for them to go.

Looking Back Down Our Eyes..

We can't look back down our own eyes,
To see who's looking out,
Or listen down our ears,
To find who's listening.

We can't smell who's smelling,
Or taste who's tasting.
We can't bite our own teeth,
Or even beat our own heart.

We can't hold our breath until we die,
Or stop our heart from beating,
Our internal organs work by themselves,
Until it's time to die.

We think we have control,
And we may have a little,
Not as much as we'd like,
Or do we have any?

Who or what is our 'puppeteer'?
What is looking out of our eyes?
Beating our heart,
And choosing when we die?

When it speaks, can we hear?
What language does it use?
Can we understand?
Can it be named?

When we sit still,
And our mind is aware and focused,
When it is sensitive and intense,
Then we can understand.

Behind the fabric of life,
Underneath the theatre,
There is a conversation,
Than doesn't use words.

Be still and hear it,
Your body talks to you,
So does the rest of the world,
In a silent language,
The one spoken by the Gods.

That which unifies everything,
IT IS ME!
I was there all the time,
I was lost and now I'm found...

Just bigger than I thought I was.....

Who Do You Train For?

Who do you train for?
Is it yourself? Or your self?
Do you train to please your Instructor?
Are you good because he says you are?

Do you 'try' to do your martial arts well?
If you're 'trying' to do something,
You're not really doing it,
You're admitting failure before you begin.

If you separate yourself from doing your art,
You're doing the opposite to what you should.
If you're training to please a separate 'self' you'll fail,
If it's to please any other person, you will always be vulnerable.

If you stop 'trying',
If you stop trying to please your self or others,
If you stop criticising your performance,
The paradox is that you will improve.

'Good' is relative, who is better?
The 'special needs' student who makes green belt after 10 years,
Or the athletically gifted student who makes black belt in 2yrs?
Is it better for us to judge or heaven?

The purpose of life is to fully engage in every moment,
You cannot do this if you are also judging,
If you stress yourself about how you de-stress,
You will never find the way.

An intelligent, engaged heart in your activity,
A fully engaged non judgemental mind,
Pure enjoyment in your actions,
Will make you the best you can be.

You Can't Stop Growing Old…

It begins when you're shaving your Dad in the mirror,
When your first steps in the morning are like the 'dawn of man' poster,
When your designer stubble makes you look homeless,
And your back goes out more than you do.

Your karate belt gets shorter,
To kick someone in the head,
You have to kick them in groin first.
When you look around the club,
Everyone is younger than you.

You're now officially 'the old boy'.
Age can be a gift or a curse,
You can either wear it with dignity,
Or act disgracefully.

No-one wants to see their granny in a mini skirt,
Or dance with their Granddad at a disco,
When the old boy throws a head kick,
To show everyone that 'he's still got it;
Everyone looks down, hoping his knees won't give way.

Thirty years of training,
Can mean thirty years of progressive study,
Or three years training repeated ten times,
Many black belts are white belts that make more noise.

Long term training should give you skill,
Grace, fluidity, power and wisdom.
It's not what you do,
But how you do it that counts.

If you've filled your martial arts bank,
With many years of skill training,
Your autumn and winter years,
Are when you reap the benefit.

We need more aged skillful people,
Too many have wasted their time,
Living from the outside in,
Instead of the inside out.

From the inside out means you have much to teach,
Knowledge that can only be gained from time and effort,
Passing it on to the next generation,
Without frustration, anger and fear.

Many people do not age,
For they are already dead.
If you make that wizened state,
Give back, so others can learn.

Armed Or Unarmed?

What came first,
The chicken or the egg?
Weapons training, or unarmed?
In martial arts it is a quest.

You would think unarmed led to weapons,
But it was most likely the other way.
Ever since man existed,
He threw rocks and used pointy sticks.

All fighting was weaponised,
Why do anything else?
The only time it became unarmed,
Was when the weapon was lost.

Village sport was wrestling,
Children in the garden wrestle,
Pups and cubs wrestle,
This made sport and play.

Why is this important?
Because martial skill begins with weapons,
Unarmed are adaptions of this,
Know the weapon, know the skill.

Weapons have to be precise,
One slip and you die.
Blades sharpen the mind,
Injury and death are always present.

Sticking, slipping, redirecting,
Cutting, slashing and stabbing,
Mobility, rooting and power,
Move seamlessly to the limbs.

Those that don't train with weapons,
Inevitably settle for less,
They play and fight like children,
Never knowing what they've missed.

Bringing Zombies To Life

Most people are zombies.
Why is this?
Because they are dead while they live,
Their body lives whilst their mind doesn't.

They live in a dormant state,
Texting while they walk,
Earphones in while they run,
Or just blank minded mouth breathers.

How can they come to life?
How can we bring that spark back?
How can they become present in the moment?
And actually live their life?

The secret is in the Dojo,
In the first commands you are given,
"Stand tall, breathe deep and focus your mind,"
The moment you do this you wake up.

Good posture awakens the body,
It becomes aware of where it is in space,
The nerves light up and feed the brain,
And now you can really breathe.

Deep breathing fills the lungs with air,
Brings oxygen into the blood,
This brings it to the brain,
And then the brain lights up.

When the mind becomes aware,
Discipline brings it to focus.
With posture it becomes sensitive,
And now it can be intense.

Time for the zombie to awake,
And live in the present,
Fear of the past and future dissipates,
As enjoyment of each moment occurs.

When you stand you are standing,
When you walk you are walking,
When you sit you are sitting,
And when you are lying down you are at ease.

For 24/7 you become alive,
Treasuring each moment,
When you move the world moves with you,
And the 'way' of martial arts is in your heart.

Treasure your live while you have it!

The Peng Balloon

Peng opens the body,
Filling it like a balloon,
Opening the joints,
And opening the soft tissue.

It opens neural, oxygen and fluid pathways,
Releasing joints tendons and muscle,
Correcting the skeletal frame,
And balancing the body.

The deep core of the body softens,
Until the feet spread evenly to the floor,
The arches fill with energy,
As they take the weight of the head.

The soften down creates the press up,
Causing the body to rise, stretch and open,
Up and out through the crown of the head,
 Until everything balances upon itself.

As the spine opens upwards,
The shoulders and arm joints open downwards,
With a soft stretch to the fingertips,
Bringing the neural system alive.

The ankles, knees and hips unlock and soften,
Opening the hips and allowing the tailbone to drop,
The chest softens and the shoulder blades settle,
Until the weight drops down the inside of the legs,
Filling the arches of the feet.

The slight press backward in the arches,
Causes the lower back to open,
The shoulder blades to part,
And the base of the skull to rise.

These four pumps then breathe energy,
Rising up the back, energising the spine and head,
The tongue then joins the top palette.
To drain it back down to the feet.

And so the cycle begins,
Each breath nourishes,
Up the back to energise,
Down the front to calm.

The natural outwards spiral in the feet,
That doesn't affect the joints,
Form a double helix at the torso,
To give a potential turn at any touch.

So the mind and body are in neutral,
But ready for any event,
With each breath the aliveness sharpens,
Making living engaged and intense.

Is Kata A Waste Of Time?

Is there a point to doing kata?
Or is it just a waste of time?
Does it have an application?
That is magical and sublime?
By the time it came from China,
To Okinawa and Japan,
It had been changed so many times,
In each and every land.

The true meaning has been lost,
And by the time it came to the West,
Nobody could remember,
As the value became less than less.

Then along came competition,
Where it just had to look good,
Nice shapes, crisp and focused,
But empty, loud and awkward.

Before internet, video and books,
People learned using mnemonics,
Remembering with rythmn and cadence,
Kata had harmonics.

Tribes used to chant,
Then they would dance to a drum,
Learning was a social event,
Where the wizened would teach the young.

Health was always important,
So posture and breath were trained,
Along with mental intent,
The young became fully engaged.

Fighting moves were too simple,
More complex skills were desired,
Life was very active and diverse,
So a complexity of skills was required.

If the warrior lost his weapon,
His opponent was still armed,
So his techniques had to be effective,
Against those that would cause great harm.

After World War Two in Japan,
Martial Arts were banned,
When Karate was finally allowed,
It was sport and empty hand.

So the reasons for kata are clear,
It is health skill and application,
Like a knot it has to be unraveled,
And studied with imagination.

Like A Never Ending Circle...

The universe is a spiral,
It's what creates time,
The energy inside is always changing,
Continually creating life.

When energy touches the spiral,
It creates the opposite force,
In movement one creates the other,
In a never ending cycle.

When you look at the yin yang symbol,
The oldest known to man,
The symbol itself is spinning,
In a three dimensional way.

The outside circle is infinite,
Because a circle never ends,
The centre line is curved,
Because of it's spiraling motion.

It is the 'Way',
Representing the journey of life,
From infinity to infinity,
Always in motion, between yin and yang.

Inside the spiral yang creates yin,
Life creates death,
Day creates night,
Male creates female.

And yin creates yang,
Death creates life,
Night creates day,
Female creates male.

This is the method of creation,
First it must have momentum,
This creates the opposite force,
Then one continually turns into the other.

The mind cannot comprehend the infinite,
It cannot see what is always there,
It can only compare one to the other,
And is blind to the underlying, infinite Way,

It cannot see it's source,
It cannot see it's destination,
It can only see what is now,
And with what it can compare.

Understanding the way it is,
Seeing the changes, feeling the 'Way',
This is the 'Grand Ultimate',
And the meaning of Tai Chi.

Putting The Egg In The Eggcup..

Putting the head in the foot,

Is like putting an egg in an eggcup.

The head is the egg,

The arch of the foot, the eggcup.

What makes the 'substantial' and 'insubstantial'?

The 'weighted leg' or 'double weighted'?

If you can feel the weight of the head in the foot,

You have to be connected through the body.

Only when the egg is in the eggcup,

Is that leg truly weighted,

The bodyline is then secure,

It is rooted, and will not tip or lean.

Mobility and power arise from good balance,

The ability to know where your body is in space,

If the head and foot are connected,

So is everything in between.

The movement of the head,

Is pumped by the arch of the foot,

Pumped from one,

To be caught by the other.

When the pump is active,
The arch flattens to the floor,
When the arch is released,
The body and head will float.

The float is still connected,
While you feel the head weight in the feet,
When one arch is down, the other is up,
This is weighted and unweighted.

This means the body is light and floating,
And can move with mobility and ease,
But because it is connected,
Any touch in any direction can be repelled.

Apart from forwards and backwards,
The head moves from side to side,
Arch to arch is on both planes,
Powering each leg even more.

The core has spiral and compression,
Giving a range of movement,
Whilst the egg is in the eggcup,
That adds a lot to the power.

So root and mobility,

Are actually just the same,

Adding to power and connectivity,

As long as the egg fits in the eggcup.

The Deepest Door..

Sit straight,

Breathe deep,

Focus the mind,

And wait for it to settle.

As moment passes to moment,

Increase the intensity,

Guard the senses,

And think without words.

The mind is the hardest muscle to train,

Weak people give up easily,

Training the body is easy,

Training the mind is the real challenge.

In stillness find the power,

Find the deepest door in your mind,

It will be protected by demons,

But when opened is the font of wisdom and power.

Your demons will always try to distract,

Other people will play on your demons,

Real power arises from intensity,

And using it to find your origin.

Therapy makes you find yourself,
Meditation realises there is no self,
There is no 'I' in the universe,
Only different shapes of the same thing.

This is he 'Way',
The deepest part of your mind,
You really are 'at one with everything',
Because you are all the same thing.

This is not a thought,
Not an emotion,
When you get there,
You will know.

Jesus spoke in parables,
The Buddha in Sutra's,
Everyone alludes to it,
Because 'the way can be spoken of is not the eternal way'.

Dig deep,
Keep going,
Don't give up,
If others found it - so can you.

Direct Transmission...

Martial arts training teach manners,
Manners and courtesy are a given,
This enables people to get along,
But then respect is earned.

Respect is a two way street,
It has to be earned both ways,
An Instructor earns the student's respect,
And the student earns that of the Instructor.

This is deeper than it first appears,
There has to be faith both ways,
Nothing is understood at first,
Until both invest time and effort.

When an Instructor gives physical correction,
Sometimes the student is too stiff to correct,
Sometimes he is too floppy,
Often his mind is not in the right place.

As time goes by the relationship develops,
Respect is earned and given,
Faith and trust develop,
And then their 'chi is in harmony'.

When their chi is in harmony,
Like dance partners they can work and move together,
Nothing is in the way,
They can 'intuit' each other.

This is called direct transmission,
The difference between 'dial up' and 'broadband',
'Jikiden' in Japanese,
'Chap Sau' in Chinese.

This 'magic' is still rare in the martial arts,
Because these days it's seen as business,
Each one thinking of what they get,
Instead of working with each other.

Respect, faith and trust,
All have to be earned,
The more you give,
The more you receive.

When you trust you can yield,
When you yield you can learn,
With nothing in the way,
The Instructor can do his work.

But respect and trust cannot be earned lightly,

It takes time and effort,

Who is prepared to put in that work?

And let the magic happen?

Eating Bitter

The Martial Arts are full of certificates and awards,

Photographs with Masters,

Everyone holding a fist up,

What's it supposed to mean?

A certificate is a piece of paper,

A belt holds up your trousers,

A photo means you met that person,

The value is what it means to you.

A grade defines the relationship,

Between student and the Instructor,

It determines what classes are attended,

And what the student is taught.

It can also define status,

The managerial structure,

Instead of foreman, manager and director,

We have sempei, sensei and renshi.

If the instructor puts too much emphasis on grades,

The students do the same,

The club becomes about certificates,

And not how the student develops.

To be concerned about grading either way,

Means you missed the point,

They should just come naturally.

The responsibility of the student is to train and improve,

The Instructor to teach and train,

When the time is right,

The Instructor gives the grade.

Death Is A Warm Blanket

Too many people fear death,
Yet it holds the key to our enlightenment,
You die many times in life,
In many different ways.

Coming from the infinite,
Then returning back,
You are joined to it all through life,
If you study 'The Way'.

You don't even know you're born,
Well actually, that's true,
Because no-one can remember it,
We become self conscious at a few years old.

So why can't we remember?
Because we are still fully connected,
And are pure universal energy,
Until someone gives us a name.

Drifting into sleep, is our name slipping away,
We commune with our unconscious,
While our name disappears,
And we can regenerate.

Meditation brings us back,
Back to where we were as a child,
The uncarved block,
Energy without a name.

The illusion of 'self',
That which is named,
Disappears when we are in harmony,
And communing with that which cannot be named.

The nameless nourishes and replenishes,
It reminds us of who we really are,
It is a place of refuge,
Reminding us from whence we came.

When it is time to return,
Death is a warm blanket,
It is from where we started,
And where we shall return.

We don't know we die,
Like we don't know when we're born,
Like we don't know when we fall asleep,
Or when we replenish in meditation.

We are born from the nameless,
We return to the nameless,
During life we replenish in the nameless,
Our name and self are illusory.

Death is a longer sleep,
It is a time of nourishment,
The universe regenerates,
And we suddenly appear again.

Once again we don the mask of self,
It is one of self awareness,
It appears and disappears throughout life,
Just for a bit of theatre.

Remember who you are,
What you were as a child,
Where you go in meditation,
The nameless is your real 'self'.

Dealing With Fear

Fear is healthy,
Everyone has it,
It keeps you on your toes,
Unless it gets out of hand.

Then it freezes you,
Or makes you into a monster,
Either way it doesn't help,
And turns you into a victim.

There is no 'quick fix',
No 'little trick' to solve it,
It requires Kung Fu,
That is time and effort.

Every day you learn to watch your emotions,
What you do and how you react,
Unnatural fear is a learned response,
That has to be unlearned.

Every time you train,
You train your emotions,
Neigong means 'inner work',
And that's where we start.

When in yin postures,
We train compassion, patience and tolerance,
When in yang,
We train courage, resolve and determination.

The mind has to stay aware and focused,
Sensitive and intense,
Intensity is the guardian,
That makes it sharp without fear.

All training must have these qualities,
Never let the intensity drop,
Never be careless or lazy,
Fear will enter into any gap.

We use the 'hunters' mindset,
To sharpen the intensity,
To take away the fear,
And just get the job done.

A martial artist is not angry,
Can always control himself,
Is not the perpetrator or victim,
A martial artist is the peacekeeper.

Are You A Fattist?

Telling a person they're fat,
And should get their lard arse of the couch,
And come down to your club or gym,
Makes you the fattist.

Every advert is about being skinny,
Every pop up on the screen,
It's a 'miracle' pill or method,
Preying on the weak.

People are overweight for many reasons,
Some have a thyroid dysfunction,
For some it's caused by medication,
And some can't move because of disability.

For some food is an addiction,
And some are emotionally disturbed,
What makes it worse for all of them,
Is that it's there for all to see.

Do you pick on the anorexic?
Do you ridicule the sick?
Do you bully the alcoholic?
And tell them to get their arse to your gym?

"Stop eating" you tell them,
Don't you think they would if they could?
Like an alcoholic can stop drinking,
Or a drug addict can stop taking drugs.

If you've always been skinny,
You may not realise the pain you cause,
An overweight person knows exactly,
What the the problem is they have.

Like any ill person,
They need understanding and help,
Not some ignorant person,
Trying to cash in on their pain.

Take care with your words and perspective,
Remember words can wound more than knives,
It's our job to help people with problems,
Not bully them with our hand in their pocket.

The Happy Button...

Happiness is a choice,

So is misery,

Happiness is a habit,

So is misery.

Which do you choose?

Which is your habit?

If you've slid into misery,

How do you change it?

Every day you should take the time,

To wake up and practice neigong (inner work),

Check out your condition,

Both mental and physical.

I have a 'happy button',

It's right there in the middle of my chest,

Not where you dirty buggars were thinking!

And I press it first thing in the morning, however I feel.

When I press it I smile,

And remember to be happy,

The choice is that simple,

Happy button – smile!

Because it's a habit,
I have to keep doing it,
Again and again throughout the day,
Happy button – smile!

Shit happens to make you miserable,
But that is on the outside,
It's your choice how you react,
And a habit strengthens the emotion.

Life is tough,
We have to be tougher,
And you can be tough,
With a smile on your face.

Happiness comes from compassion,
It comes from giving,
It comes from being a friend,
And a smile is infectious.

Some people light a room when they enter,
Some when they leave,
When people see you do they smile?
Or think "here comes that miserable sod?"

Your choice, it's that simple,

Press the happy button and smile,

Again and again, until it's your nature,

This simple trick can change your life.

The Learning Process

The learning process of the mind,
Is a specific process,
It is important to understand,
To be able to learn effectively.

Shi Kon use a mnemonic acronym,
As this is the best way to remember,
If you refine this process,
All learning will be easier.

The acronym we use is ATARC,
This is a specific order,
One cannot be done effectively,
Without the preparation of the other.

A is for attitude,
This is the most important,
Unless this is in the correct state,
Everything else will be wrong.

Attitude is emotional intelligence,
Putting nothing in the way of learning,
If you think you can't, you can't,
And if you think you can, you can.

Bowing as you enter the training area,

Is the most important task,

Clearing the mind of all its junk,

And preparing to learn without hindrance.

T is for thought,

Taking in the correct information,

Then planning the movement,

Planning and preparation mean you know what you are about to do.

A is for action,

Action is the result of attitude and thought,

In itself it is pure,

And unhindered at the time.

R is for refection,

Looking back to see if it was right,

Applying attitude and thought,

Were they physically enacted?

C is for correction,

It is easy to make it worse,

Correct attitude, thought or action,

By changing the correct thing the correct way.

The chain is a powerful tool,
If you understand its use,
Developed as a learning process,
It empowers and corrects itself.

Learning how to learn,
Putting nothing in the way,
And understanding the process.
Changes everything forever.

Principles And Dynamics

What is the difference between principles and dynamics?
Both underlay technique,
Principles are present all the time,
But dynamics change and combine.

The feet must always be in the right place,
At the right time and press the right way,
The body must always be aligned,
And the mind always alert, focused, sensitive and intense.

The breathing must always be deep and natural,
The internal line always connected,
The spine and core always being manipulated,
And the ideas of wedging and spiraling always in place.

These principles are what make a technique work,
Combined they give immense power,
Break one and the others fold,
They give the strategy to win or lose.

Whilst keeping these in place,
There are strategies you can use,
These will come and go,
And dynamically change the game.

Ward off is to repel the opponent without losing structure,

Roll back is to lead the opponent into nothingness,

Press to smother and repel not allowing to opponent to attack,

Push is to uproot bouncing the opponent out of his feet.

Bump is to hit and uproot by bumping with the body mass,

Strike is to hit with body parts like fist and elbow supported by body mass.

Pluck is to shake or vibrate to break structure.

Split is to take the opponent in two opposing circles at the same time.

These can be combined with standing firm to repel,

Or stepping in to attack,

Stepping back to absorb,

Or to the side to evade or deflect.

The 8 principles are always present,

The 13 dynamics are interchangeably used within their frame,

And the techniques are the method of expressing them.

What Happened?

When I was a child and teenager in the 50's and 60's,

The public owned it's own services,

Trains, buses, electric, gas, water and mail,

And the profit helped pay for community services.

Prescriptions and university education were free,

Legal and union representation gave job security,

Council housing and rent control meant everyone was housed,

Equality was becoming a reality.

With free education, social mobility truly happened,

We had 2 Prime ministers from grammar school education,

Anyone from anywhere could become anything,

At last society was moving forwards and there was hope.

Computers and machinery were designed to ease the burden,

We were told soon we would be working a 20hour week,

And earning more money with more leisure,

Science was going to improve the quality of life.

Our bank manager was our trusted friend,

He had our interests at heart,

Companies valued loyalty,

The longer you were a customer, the better deals you received.

Policeman walked the beat and were our friends,
They represented and defended the community,
Teachers educated our children,
And doctors would see us anytime and care.

Now our politicians are all privately educated,
Our country and services have been sold,
Our sick, disabled and disenfranchised are persecuted,
All care and compassion has dissolved.

Our minds and fears are constantly distracted,
We look at boobs and bums and blame the immigrants,
The rich have got richer and the poor poorer,
The 1% have it all.

We eat shit, take shit, and believe shit,
Pay through the nose for what was ours,
The poor blame the poorer,
While the rich laugh up their sleeve.

The police, NHS and education,
Just fill in forms,
They massage the figures,
To keep us in the dark.

We have no representation,
Not at any level anywhere,
As the poor get squeezed yet again,
Violence will arise.

We sold weapons to all sides of global conflict,
We caused most of the wars,
Yet we complain about refugees,
And one day this will backfire.

Until we find compassion,
Until we really care,
Until we lift the blindfolds,
We will repeat history.

Millions are slaughtered in conflict,
Millions are refugees and starving,
Billions of animals are slaughtered,
And we're still looking at tits and bums.

When will humanity wake up?

Seeing With Clarity

That precious moment when you 'wake up' from meditation,
When all behind the mask is revealed,
When you see things with total clarity,
And the circus that's always been there.

Can you imagine if we invented roads now?
Tarmac strips between pedestrians without barriers,
Jagged pieces of metal travelling at 70 mph,
With people dodging between.

Women with painted faces,
Teetering along on pointy shoe stilts,
Making themselves look like circus clowns,
Matching the image of the ringmasters media.

Men wearing a gaily coloured hangman's noose around their neck,
With a 'manscaped' face, and their wife's tight trousers,
Walking like a gym made balloon man,
With a bottle stuck up their backside..

People performing for the Ringmaster,
To buy things they don't need,
Made by foreign slave labour,
Poisoning the environment with their greed.

A third of humanity starving,
Two thirds in abject poverty,
The 3rd world slaughtering each other,
While the first world is obese.

150 billion animals slaughtered annually,
For food we don't need,
The pain, torture and suffering,
Behind closed doors so we don't see.

People living from the outside in,
Instead of the inside out,
Performing to please others,
Never becoming who they should.

A planet being poisoned by its circus,
Waiting patiently to burn down the tents,
The planet doesn't die, it just changes,
The circus kills itself.

The colours, music and make up,
Distract from what's really going on,
The Ringmaster thinks only of profit,
And the clown's shoes are too big for his feet.

It's Yesterday No More

What you think you were yesterday,
You weren't.
What you think you are today,
You're not.

Memories are false,
They're what you want to make them.
If you're troubled,
You think they're bad.

If you're happy,
You think they were good,
But everyone there will see them different,
Just like witnesses at a crime scene.

What you were and what you are now is not true,
It's just your opinion,
What you did or didn't do,
Is being judged by someone who is biased.

Biased by culture, plagued by guilt,
Sometimes hurt that is hidden,
Festering in a mental cupboard,
Arising when you're drunk or sad.

What is good in one culture, is bad in another,

What is considered right in one age, is wrong in another,

Religion is always good, the politics of them are bad.

Wise teachings skewed for purpose by politicians.

The past is gone and now doesn't exist,

Cut the cord and let it go.

Every day you are born again,

And can make a clean start.

Tainted by the past is bad.

Wizened by the past is good.

Withdraw the knife and heal,

Don't keep stabbing yourself with it.

When we injure the body,

We take care of it and heal,

When we injure the emotions,

We keep doing it again and again.

So cut that cord and let it go,

Allow yourself to heal,

Do something positive,

And become a good person.

When you let go the light is brighter,
Colours are more vibrant,
The air is fresher,
And every day is good.

Diversity and Compassion...

I was brought up in the streets of South London,
Worked in the Fire Brigade and security teams,
Also on road laying gangs,
And then in the Martial Arts.

Always with groups of men,
We ridiculed everyone, including ourselves,
If we didn't like someone,
We hit them.

Do you want a slap?
Give him a dig,
Don't like him,
Knock him out.

That was our reaction to everything,
Like children spitting their dummies,
Losing intelligence and getting angry,
Then just wanting to hurt someone.

It was natural to insult everyone,
Different colour, different size,
Different gender or gay,
Everyone was a target.

Even my friends names reflected our culture,
Ginger, Blackie, Chalkie, Legless, Fatty and Slim,
If you didn't ridicule yourself,
Someone will do it for you.

Different times, different rules, different culture.
But that wasn't me, it was the 'blind' assumptions I grew up with,
My family, school, friends and work made me who I was,
If I didn't meditate to change, I would still be the same.

I realised that you don't need to love everyone,
You don't even have to like them,
To be kind and patient with them,
And treat them with compassion.

You don't need to agree with someone,
For them to be your friend,
They don't need to be like you,
For you to learn from them.

When you dislike someone,
Is it them or is it you?
Compassion opens doors,
And from empathy you learn.

Diversity and empathy is what makes us better,
It makes us rise above being heathen,
Throw away the pitchforks and flaming torches,
Listen, learn and grow.

When the fear stops,
When the aggression abates,
When we can work with others,
The media control loses power.

We have to care for others,
Or being human was a waste,
We have to think for ourselves,
To become an emotionally intelligent race.

And only then will the world become a better place.

You'll Have To Kill Me…

The only way you'll stop me is to kill me.

I don't give up.

If I gave up I might just as well be dead.

Because life will have no value for me.

This makes me pick my battles carefully,

I won't pick a fight just because I'm angry,

Or disappointed, or any other shallow reason,

Every challenge is one that I am prepared to dedicate my life to.

There is only win or die,

Nothing in between,

Every thought, movement and technique has this dedication,

Not desperate, but resolute and determined.

Starting on the path of martial arts,

For me was not a 'social' decision,

It wasn't 'something to do',

It was beginning a transformation.

I will not fail again,

I will not lose again,

I will do whatever is required,

Win or die.

I may lose a battle,
But I won't lose a war,
I only lose if I stop.
So I won't stop.

I will play the long game,
Anything worth having,
Doesn't come easily,
I'm always ready for a war of attrition.

I practice and study more that anyone else,
My body is ready,
My mind is ready,
I am always as prepared as I can be.

I don't waste my time,
I don't waste my money,
I only use what I really need,
The rest is ready for battle.

I watch any potential opponent,
I see their strengths and weaknesses,
I note their vulnerabilities,
Always ready to go for the kill.

The greatest victory,

Is where there is no fight,

Where you defeat the opponent with your mind,

The mind is the hardest 'muscle' in the body to train.

The 'warrior way' is long term victory,

To be determined when others give up,

To always challenge adversity,

And not stop until death.

Three Essentials To Enlightenment

If you want to be enlightened,

And that doesn't mean in the hippie sense,

But to unburden yourself from too much suffering,

There are 3 essentials that will help.

The first is knowledge,

To become the one that knows,

Some people get this through experience and study,

And some just never do.

Knowledge gives a broad perspective,

It helps you follow the right path,

Books, learning and listening give knowledge,

Intelligent use of them makes you grow.

Study, meditation and experience,

Are three keys to learning,

The way of the true warrior,

Is the pen, stillness and the sword.

Knowledge is very helpful,

But only if it leads to truth,

Discovering truth and how it manifests,

Is the second essential to grow.

Truth is always there and always the same,
There is no 'your' or 'my' truth,
Because it just is,
When seen, it always works.

The search for truth means no distraction,
You cannot be lazy or apathetic,
Never take anyone's word,
But always discover for yourself.

Politics, media and business,
Always want to distract,
To give themselves power over you,
They cannot afford the truth.

The truth sets you free.
When seen it cannot be unseen.
The confusion in life is visible,
When the veil is lifted.

The third essential is friendship,
Others on your path,
Choose your friends wisely,
And bonded you are strong.

We are a communal species,
We work well as a group,
Isolation make us scared and lonely,
Making us prey for social predators.

When we join together,
Seeking knowledge and truth,
We evolve into something better,
And the burden of life is lifted.

Becoming the one that knows,
Following the path of truth,
Joining together in friendship,
Is the triple gem of wisdom.

Taking Or Giving?

Not being a liability on others,

Means you always pay your bills,

Living within your means,

And not spending like a fool.

Modern society tries to make you a slave,

The media want you to spend,

To buy things you don't need,

And to owe your life to them.

You have things that work and serviceable,

Yet you always want more or new,

Because you are hypnotised by others,

Who want to own your soul.

Taking responsibility for your purse,

Is a part of taking responsibility for your self,

Taking possession of your time,

And preventing your control by others.

It's important to earn a living,

By not causing any harm,

And then by benefitting others,

Giving, instead of taking.

The question often arises,
Should a club be for profit,
Whether amateur or professional,
It should always pay its bills.

A club is always 'business',
However it is run,
The question is as always,
Does it do good or harm?

So how do you earn your living?
Do you cause good or harm?
Do you benefit your community?
Or are you a parasite on their back?

Does spending make you feel good?
Buying things you do not need?
Are you killing the planet and people?
By feeding your weakness and greed?

The balance of earning and spending,
Is basic maths at best,
Yet so many are fooled by business,
And live life their life in debt.

Because our life is short,
'Ownership' is a farce,
We only care for anything,
On a fully repairing lease.

Quicken the pace of the planet,
By consuming more than you need,
Is only spoiling it for your children,
With your own interminable greed.

It's Not What You Do

What's the best fighting style?
What's the best art for self defence?
That art is not effective!
Why waste your time with those techniques?

We all like to judge,
And looking at those judging,
My first thought is,
People in glass houses….

My second thought is,
You're looking at it the wrong way round,
It's not what you do,
It's how you do it that counts.

It's not the art,
It's not the style,
It's the person training,
That makes the difference.

I know great fighters,
That have never done martial arts,
They have a heart and spirit,
That surpass many that do.

I know many classical martial artists,

That practice technique and kata,

That the RBSD people abhor,

Yet make what they do work in the street.

There are those that have got it,

And those that haven't,

Those that are judgmental,

Usually don't have what it takes.

They distract everyone,

By making lots of noise,

Trying to convince everyone,

That they know what they're talking about.

They wear the uniform,

Camouflaging their fear,

With fierce expressions,

And a CV by Enid Blyton.

Those that have what it takes,

Don't need to brag,

Don't need to threaten,

Because they can do the business.

A rich man doesn't need to display his wealth,
A powerful man is usually polite,
A successful man feels secure,
And doesn't need to bully others.

The only time to look down to someone,
Is when you are helping them up,
You never make yourself look bigger,
By making others look smaller.

Be truthful about what you've done,
Be humble in your approach,
Always respect others,
And help them when you can.

Why Me?

Why me?
I'm a good person,
I don't do anything wrong,
So why do I have to suffer?

All the horrible evil people in the world,
And this has to happen to me,
That can't be right,
Is there no justice?

Do you think there is a God sitting in judgment of you?
That people that do good get a 'nice' time?
A God making sure that evil people suffer?
Look around you….

There is the law of the universe,
That is true,
Then there is a current law of society,
That is attempted by humans.

It is cultural, founded in religion,
Devised by politicians,
Intended to make people live in peace,
It often fails.

Human law won't stop you getting cancer,
It won't prevent sickness or accidents,
It won't stop wars, floods or earthquakes,
It's designed to help people live in peace.

Even that doesn't work all the time,
It's not usually there when crime happens,
It only tries to clean up afterwards,
So justice has limited effect.

It is a cultural way of thinking,
That we 'deserve' a good or bad time,
It is false and wrong,
And will create a victim mentality.

There is cause and effect,
We can work with that,
But what happens, happens,
And we have to deal with that.

If we develop warriors mind,
Good and bad are the same,
We work with what we get,
And always make the best.

We don't look at others,
With envy, greed or jealousy,
They have their own problems,
No one gets away free.

If they did, what's the point of being alive?

Learning Friendship..

If you want good friends,
You have to learn how to be a good friend,
It's a two way street,
And good friendship is life's treasure.

Martial arts training brings people together,
People of a like mind,
Wanting to improve themselves,
Together you bleed, laugh and cry.

Over the years, some will go wrong,
But you cannot let one person,
Make you into a twat like them,
Remain true and others will take their place.

Make acquaintances easily but not friends,
Earning respect takes time,
The better person you become,
The better friends you will have.

Friendship takes effort,
It can never be one sided,
But good bonded friends,
Can take on the world.

If you have no friends,

It's not the fault of others,

And if you think everyone else is an idiot,

It's probably you.

The Secret Of Internal Power

The Secret Of Internal Power,

Is in the spine and body core,

Learn how to manipulate these,

And you will have great natural power.

There 4 pairs of spine and core skills,

Understand them in the neigong,

Learn them in the qigong,

And then apply them in technique.

Soften and connect,

Open and close,

Stretch and compress,

Twist and release.

One normally follows the other,

But you release after every skill,

A release can be fast or slow,

When you release you always then soften and connect.

There are a multitude of ways to pulse,

Sending energy to the edge,

Into the opponent to disrupt,

Without breaking your own structure.

This is a secret,
But no one will know it,
Until they have put in the time and effort,
To really grasp these words.

Printed in Great Britain
by Amazon

27644611R00066